KELLY CLARKSON
ALL I EVER WANTED

ISBN 978-1-4234-8132-4

HAL•LEONARD®
CORPORATION
7777 W. BLUEMOUND RD. P.O. BOX 13819 MILWAUKEE, WI 53213

MY LIFE WOULD SUCK WITHOUT YOU

Words and Music by LUKASZ GOTTWALD,
MAX MARTIN and CLAUDE KELLY

Up-beat Pop

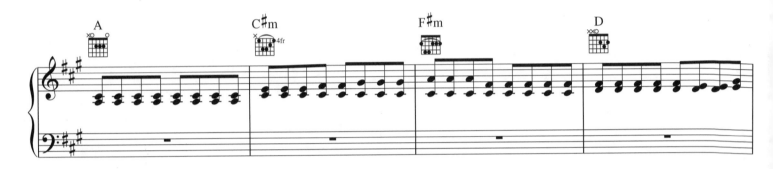

Guess this means ___ you're sor - ry,   you're
May - be I ___ was stu - pid   for

stand - ing at ___ my door. ___   Guess this means ___ you take ___
tell - ing you ___ good - bye. ___   May - be I ___ was wrong ___

I DO NOT HOOK UP

Words and Music by GREG WELLS,
KARA DioGUARDI and KATY PERRY

CRY

Words and Music by KELLY CLARKSON,
JASON HALBERT and MARK LEE TOWNSEND

If an-y-one asks, I'll tell them we've both just moved
I'll tell them we just grew a-

on. When peo-ple all stare, I pre-tend
part. Yeah, what do I care

that I don't hear them talk.
if they be-lieve me or not?

DON'T LET ME STOP YOU

Words and Music by JOSEF LAROSSI,
ANDREAS ROMDHANE, CLAUDE KELLY
and MATS VALENTIN

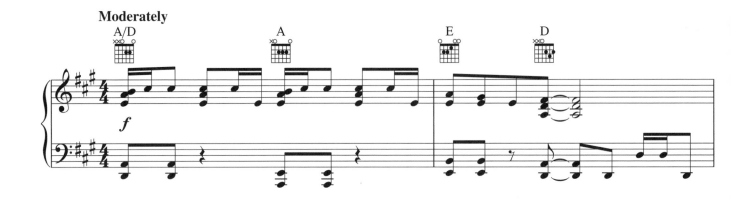

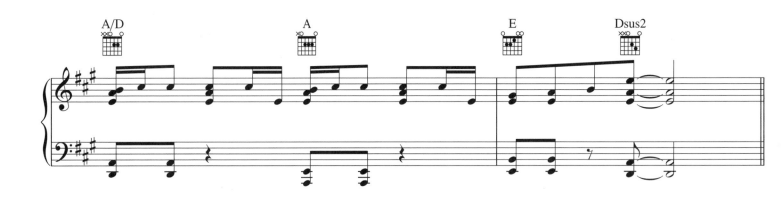

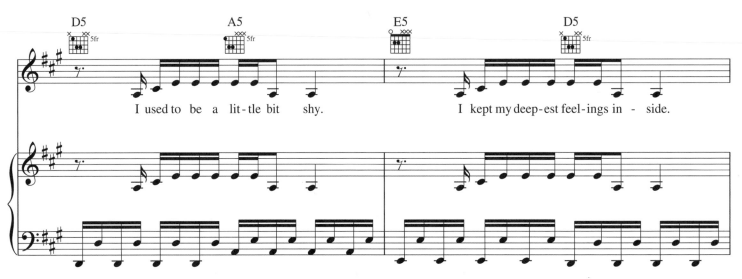

I used to be a lit-tle bit shy.   I kept my deep-est feel-ings in - side.

ALL I EVER WANTED

Words and Music by SAMUEL WATTERS,
LOUIS IANCANIELLO and DAMEON ARANDA

Moderately

Tear up the pho - to - graphs, but yes - ter - day __ won't let go, __
I'd rath - er walk __ a - lone; don't wan - na chase __ you a - round __

ev - 'ry day, ev - 'ry day, ev - 'ry min - ute.

Here comes the emp - ti - ness; just can't be lone - ly a - lone, __
I'd fall a thou - sand times 'fore I'd let __ you drag me down, __

* Recorded a half step higher.

All I ever wanted, all I ever wanted was an

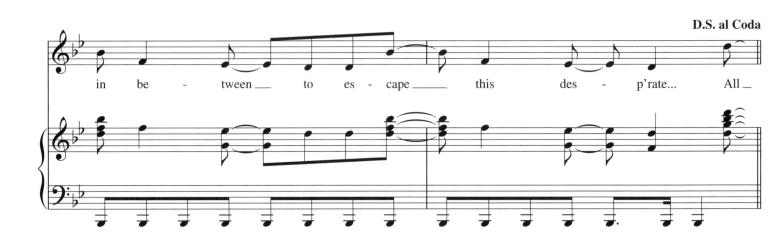

in be-tween to es-cape this des-p'rate... All

I ev-er want-ed was you.

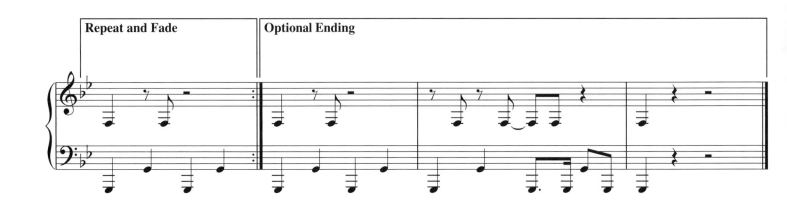

ALREADY GONE

Words and Music by KELLY CLARKSON
and RYAN TEDDER

Re-mem-ber all the things we want-ed. Now all our mem-o-ries, they're haunt-ed.
but I know that you'll find an-oth-er

We were al-ways meant to say good-bye. ___
that does-n't al-ways make you wan-na cry. ___

IF I CAN'T HAVE YOU

Words and Music by KELLY CLARKSON
and RYAN TEDDER

SAVE YOU

Words and Music by RYAN TEDDER
and AIMEE PROAL

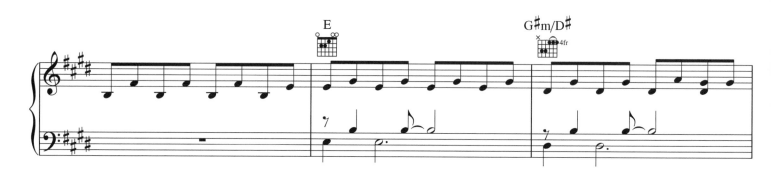

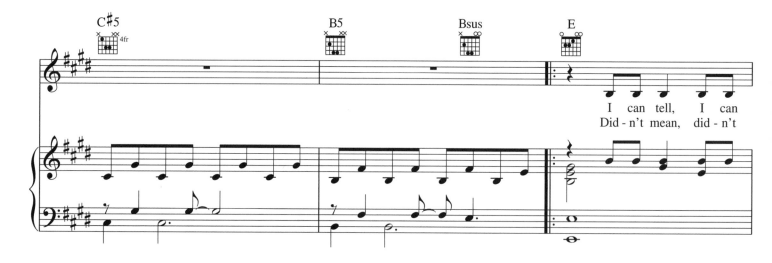

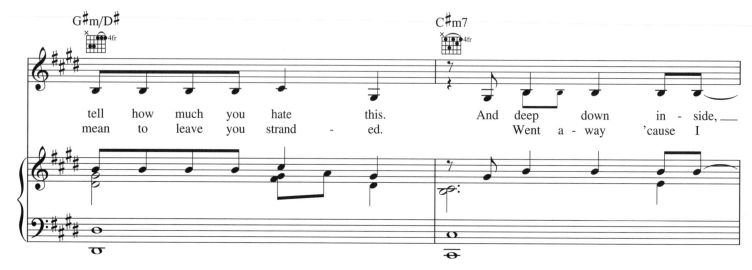

WHYYAWANNABRINGMEDOWN

Words and Music by SAMUEL WATTERS,
LOUIS BIANCANIELLO and DAMEON ARANDA

LONG SHOT

Words and Music by GLEN BALLARD,
MATT THIESEN and KATY PERRY

IMPOSSIBLE

Words and Music by KELLY CLARKSON
and RYAN TEDDER

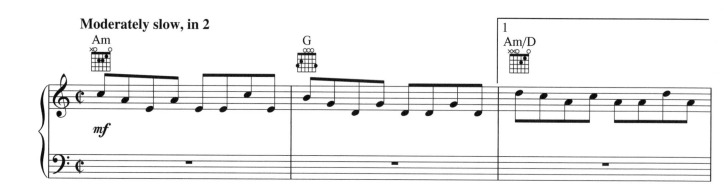

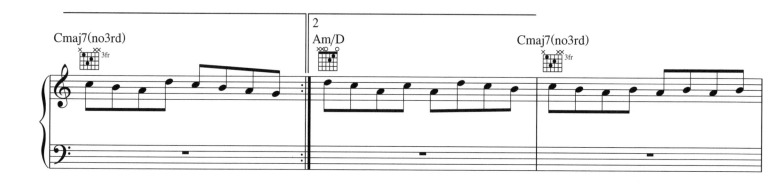

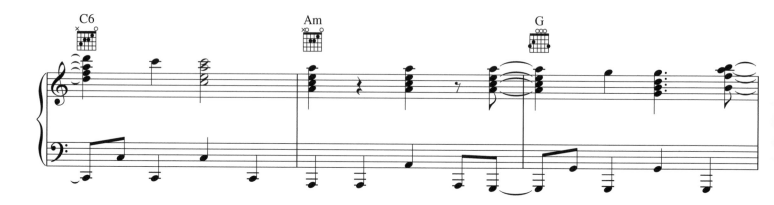

READY

Words and Music by KELLY CLARKSON
and RYAN TEDDER

* *Recorded a half step lower.*

I WANT YOU

Words and Music by KELLY CLARKSON
and JOAKIM AHLUND

walk-ing to-geth - er, _____ screw-ing up, for worse or for bet - ter.

You, you, you, you, ___ you, you, you. I, I, I, I, I, I,

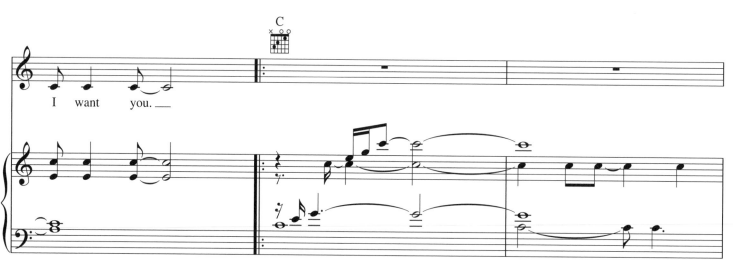

I want you. ___

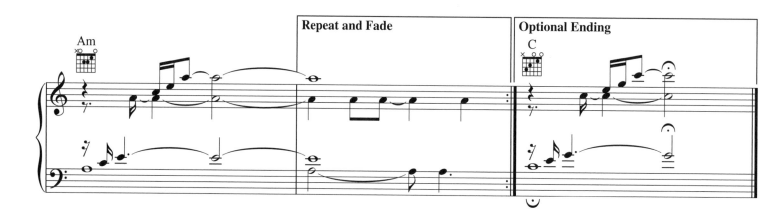

Repeat and Fade

Optional Ending

IF NO ONE WILL LISTEN

Words and Music by
KERI NOBLE

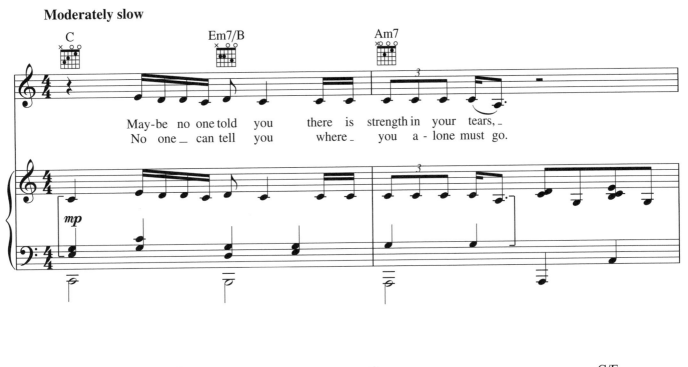

May-be no one told you there is strength in your tears,
No one _ can tell you where _ you a - lone must go.

and so you fight _ to keep from pour - ing out. _
There's no tell - ing what you'll find ___ there. ___

But what if you un - lock the gate _ that keeps your sec - ret soul? Do you
and God _ I know _ the fear _ that eats a - way at your bones; it's